Troy Public Library
510 W. Big Beaver Rd.
Troy, MI 48084

MW01477979

NOVEMBER
2016

FUN FACT FILE: ANIMAL ADAPTATIONS

20 FUN FACTS ABOUT BIRD ADAPTATIONS

By Sarah Machajewski

Gareth Stevens
PUBLISHING

Please visit our website, www.garethstevens.com. For a free color catalog of all our high-quality books, call toll free 1-800-542-2595 or fax 1-877-542-2596.

Cataloging-in-Publication Data

Names: Machajewski, Sarah.
Title: 20 fun facts about bird adaptations / Sarah Machajewski.
Description: New York : Gareth Stevens Publishing, 2016. | Series: Fun fact file: animal adaptations | Includes index.
Identifiers: ISBN 9781482444483 (pbk.) | ISBN 9781482443929 (6 pack) | ISBN 9781482444308 (library bound)
Subjects: LCSH: Birds–Juvenile literature. | Birds–Behavior–Juvenile literature.
Classification: LCC QL676.2 M28 2016 | DDC 597–dc23

First Edition

Published in 2017 by
Gareth Stevens Publishing
111 East 14th Street, Suite 349
New York, NY 10003

Copyright © 2017 Gareth Stevens Publishing

Designer: Andrea Davison-Bartolotta
Editor: Kristen Nelson

Photo credits: Cover, p. 1 Joseph Scott Photography/Shutterstock.com; p. 4 Hugh Lansdown/Shutterstock.com; p. 5 (top left) Sergey Uryadnikov/Shutterstock.com; p. 5 (top right) claffra/Shutterstock.com; p. 5 (middle left) Joshua Raif/Shutterstock.com; p. 5 (middle right) Nazzu/Shutterstock.com; p. 5 (bottom left) Alta Oosthuizen/Shutterstock.com; p. 5 (bottom right) Butterfly Hunter/Shutterstock.com; p. 6 44kmos/Shutterstock.com; p. 7 Andrzej Kubik/Shutterstock.com; p. 8 (inset) Robert L Kothenbeutel/Shutterstock.com; p. 8 (main) Christopher MacDonald/Shutterstock.com; p. 9 Lori Labrecque/Shutterstock.com; p. 10 Targn Pleiades/Shutterstock.com; p. 11 (flight) Nejron Photo/Shutterstock.com; p. 11 (tail) Ian Duffield/Shutterstock.com; p. 11 (contour) Roberto Garcia/Shutterstock.com; p. 11 (semiplume) schankz/Shutterstock.com; p. 11 (down) CuorerouC/iStock/Thinkstock; p. 11 (filoplume) Lori Skelton/Shutterstock.com; p. 11 (bristle) johannviloria/Shutterstock.com; p. 12 Art Wittingen/Shutterstock.com; p. 13 Natalia Khalaman/Shutterstock.com; p. 14 veleknez/Shutterstock.com; p. 15 Panu Ruangjan/Shutterstock.com; p. 16 Eduard Kyslynskyy/Shutterstock.com; p. 17 Eric Isselee/Shutterstock.com; p. 18 visceralimage/Shutterstock.com; p. 19 (left) Anne Montfort/Photononstop/Getty Images; p. 19 (right) Visuals Unlimited, Inc./Gregory Basco/Visuals Unlimited/Getty Images; p. 20 (top) Tania Thomson/Shutterstock.com; p. 20 (bottom) Robin Keefe/Shutterstock.com; p. 21 Tom Murphy/National Geographic Magazines/Getty Images; p. 22 pr2is/Shutterstock.com; p. 23 Tim Laman/National Geographic Magazines/Getty Images; p. 24 Tom Franks/Shutterstock.com; p. 25 Vishnevskiy Vasily/Shutterstock.com; p. 26 Arto Hakola/Shutterstock.com; p. 27 zizar/Shutterstock.com; p. 28 Rahul Alvares/Shutterstock.com; p. 29 Paul Nicklen/National Geographic/Getty Images.

All rights reserved. No part of this book may be reproduced in any form without permission in writing from the publisher, except by a reviewer.

Printed in the United States of America

CPSIA compliance information: Batch #CS16GS: For further information contact Gareth Stevens, New York, New York at 1-800-542-2595.

Contents

Birds Around the World 4
Big, Small—and Hidden! 6
Fantastic Feathers 10
Wingin' It 14
Beaks and Feet 18
Dazzling Displays 22
"Cheep Cheep" 24
Mighty Migrations 26
Look Around You 28
Glossary 30
For More Information 31
Index 32

Words in the glossary appear in **bold** type the first time they are used in the text.

Birds Around the World

Look at the sky, a tree, your backyard, or your windowsill. In any of these places, you may see a bird! There are about 10,000 different species, or kinds, of birds, and they live everywhere. They're found in our neighborhoods and in wild places, too.

Birds that live in one place aren't always found in another. How do birds around the world survive? They have adaptations, or changes that help them survive in their **habitat**. The adaptations affect how they look and act.

Adaptations appear slowly over thousands and thousands of years. Birds with a special adaptation pass it on to their young, who then pass it on to their young.

5

Big, Small—and Hidden!

FACT 1

The world's smallest bird is only 2 inches (5.1 cm) long and weighs less than a dime.

The bee hummingbird's size allows it to visit tiny flowers bigger birds don't bother with. It doesn't have to **compete** with them for food, so it always has enough to eat.

From the smallest to the biggest, all birds have special adaptations that help them survive best where they live.

FACT 2

The world's largest bird can grow to be 9 feet (2.7 m) tall!

The ostrich's long legs help it run from danger. Predators can't catch this bird when it's running more than 45 miles (72 km) per hour!

FACT 3

Snowy owls get whiter as they get older.

White feathers help snowy owls blend in with their snow-covered habitat. This helps with hunting, since **prey** can't see them. Snowy owls eat up to 1,600 small animals called lemmings each year.

Some birds have colors that seem rather boring. But they're an important adaptation. They don't stand out, which means birds can stay safe—and alive.

FACT 4

The eastern screech owl looks like tree bark.

Eastern screech owls have grey-brown feathers with bands of spots and stripes. Predators can't tell where the owl is when it's sitting among tree branches. When an animal blends in with its surroundings like this, it's called camouflage.

Fantastic Feathers

FACT 5

Birds have seven kinds of feathers, each with a special job!

Wing feathers lift birds in the air. Tail feathers steer during flight. Contour feathers keep the body dry. Semiplume and down feathers trap heat. Filoplumes act as feelers, while bristles **protect** the eyes and face.

7 Feathers of the Bird World

wing: air moves under and over the feather, creating lift

tail: helps birds steer during flight

contour: gives birds shape and size; keeps water away from the body

semiplume: found between other feathers; helps trap heat near the body

down: soft, fluffy feathers trap heat near the body

filoplume: act as feelers; possibly help birds sense what the other feathers are doing

bristle: protect birds' eyes and face

Each kind of feather is specially shaped for its job.

Some birds make preening oil in a body part near their tail. They spread it over their feathers with their beak. It keeps the feathers healthy and waterproof.

FACT 6

Birds can have up to 25,000 feathers!

Birds take lots of time to care for their feathers. When a bird cleans its feathers with its beak, it's called preening. It keeps feathers in place, which makes for a smooth flight. Preening also removes dust, dirt, and tiny bugs.

FACT 7

Birds replace their feathers at least once a year.

Molting is when birds shed their feathers and grow new ones. The new feathers might be brightly colored to **attract** a **mate**. They might be thicker to stay warm during winter or thinner to keep cool in summer.

Wingin' It

FACT 8

Turkeys can fly quickly to a nearby tree, but won't be seen high in the sky.

The shape of a bird's wings affects how it flies. Short, round wings, like a turkey's, are good for getting in the air quickly. Wide, flat wings are made for **soaring**.

Turkeys' feathers offer camouflage in the forests where they live.

All About Wings

elliptical wings:
short and round
good for short bursts of flying
can't be used to fly long distances
examples: blackbirds, sparrows, crows, robins

high-speed wings:
long, thin, and pointy
good for flying fast
can maintain speed over long distances
examples: falcons, ducks, swifts

passive soaring wings:
long and wide
good for catching and riding the wind
have "finger feathers" on the tips, which help change direction
examples: eagles, hawks, storks

active soaring wings:
long and narrow
good for gliding on the wind
good for slow flight
examples: gulls, albatrosses, gannets

There are four main types of wings. Some birds have wings that fall in between these major groups.

Bird bones may be light, but they're also strong. That's because they're fused, or joined, together. This helps the bones stand up to the forces of taking off, flying, landing, and more.

FACT 9

A bird's bones weigh less than all the feathers that cover its body.

Birds' bones are hollow, which means they're empty on the inside. They also have fewer bones than other animals. A light **skeleton** makes flying easier.

FACT 10

A bird's head makes up less than 1 percent of its body weight.

Birds don't have the added weight of lots of teeth. How do they eat their food, then? They have a special stomach called a gizzard that grinds food once it's inside their body.

Beaks and Feet

FACT 11

Hooked beaks help raptors rip apart their prey.

Raptors, such as eagles and falcons, hunt prey that's too big to be swallowed whole. They use their sharp, hooked beak to tear flesh into bite-sized pieces.

FACT 12

Toucans use their 7.5-inch (19 cm) bill to throw fruit.

Toucans use their bill to grab fruit from hard-to-reach branches. Then, they toss the fruit in the air, tip their head back, and swallow. Toucans also throw fruit to each other during mating.

pelican

Bird beaks, or bills, come in many shapes and sizes. Short, fat beaks help crack seeds, while wide, deep beaks are perfect for scooping up fish!

FACT 13

Herons have long toes that keep them balanced.

Herons walk slowly near the water's edge, looking for food below the water's surface. Their long toes spread their weight over a large area, so they stay balanced when walking through soft mud.

duck feet

A bird's feet can tell you something special about how it lives. Swans, ducks, and geese have webbed feet that act like paddles in the water.

FACT 14

Robins lock their feet in place so they don't fall over while sleeping.

Robins can't lie down, so they rest upright. When they stand on something, the **tendons** in their feet tighten. The feet don't **relax** until the bird takes flight.

Robins also have a long back toe that helps them grip the branch they're on.

Dazzling Displays

FACT 15

Male peacocks use their giant, brightly colored tail to attract a mate.

Female peacocks are attracted to males with big, colorful tails. Studies have shown they prefer tails with eye-shaped spots to other shapes, so males with these spots have a better chance at mating.

Attracting a mate through dance is called a display. A wild, attention-grabbing display shows females that a male is the best, strongest partner to choose. Sometimes, the female joins in!

FACT 16

To find a mate, birds of paradise have to dance.

Males move their body, dive, hang upside down, puff out their feathers, and make a lot of **commotion** to get females' attention. Young birds learn how to do this dance by watching older birds!

"Cheep Cheep"

FACT 17

Male mockingbirds may learn around 200 songs in their lifetime.

Mockingbirds are always learning new sounds. They mock, or copy, birdcalls, frog sounds, car alarms, and more. They use their song to find a mate, claim territory, and warn predators to stay away.

Baby birds are noisy when they're hungry. Their begging calls get their parents' attention. However, all the noise may tell predators where they are.

FACT 18

Birds use different calls for different reasons.

Birds can change their calls to tell others who they are, where they are, where the food is, and if danger is near. Each species has its own call, and birds use it to find each other.

Mighty Migrations

FACT 19

The Arctic tern travels about 18,640 miles (30,000 km) a year!

This bird flies from its home in the Arctic Circle to Antarctica and back each year. It doesn't have to look hard for food—large bodies of water are a great source of fish.

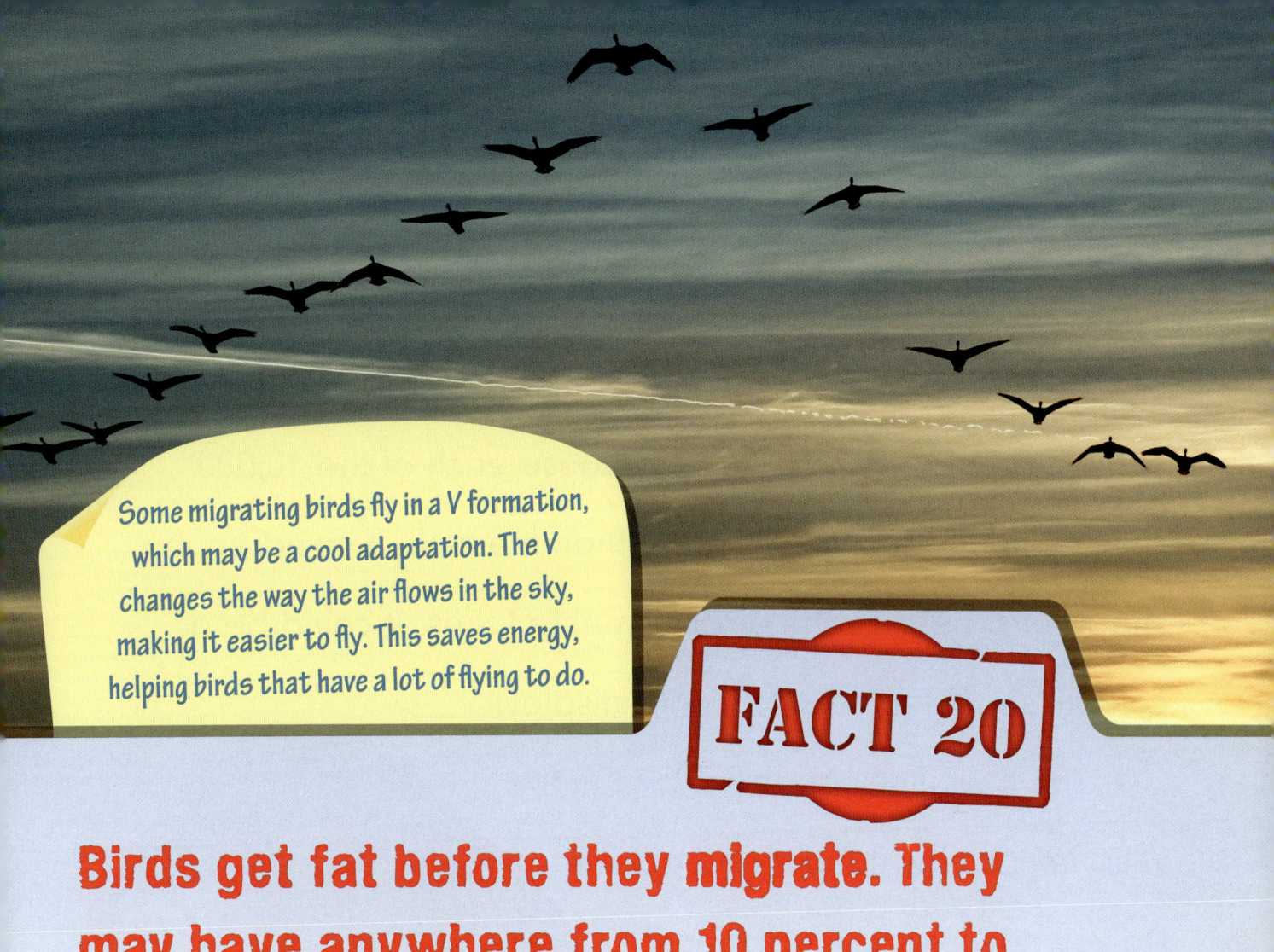

Some migrating birds fly in a V formation, which may be a cool adaptation. The V changes the way the air flows in the sky, making it easier to fly. This saves energy, helping birds that have a lot of flying to do.

FACT 20

Birds get fat before they migrate. They may have anywhere from 10 percent to 100 percent body fat.

Fat contains the **energy** birds need to fly long distances.

Some birds gain weight by eating fruit instead of bugs.

They burn off the fat as they fly.

Look Around You

Bird adaptations are some of the most interesting in the entire animal kingdom. That's because each of the 10,000 species has something different than the next. It could be the shape of a beak or the arrangement of toes. It could be a colorful set of feathers or a wild display!

The next time you see a bird in the wild, notice how it looks and acts. Do you notice any adaptations? What can they tell you about the bird?

Emperor penguins' bodies are shaped so they can move through the water easily when they dive deep for food.

Glossary

attract: to cause someone or something to have interest

commotion: a state of noisy activity

compete: to try to win something by being better at it than others

energy: the power to do work

habitat: the natural place where an animal or plant lives

mate: one of two animals that come together to produce babies. Also, to come together to make babies.

migrate: to move to warmer or colder places for a season

prey: an animal that is hunted by other animals for food

protect: to keep safe

relax: to soften

skeleton: the frame that supports an animal's body

soar: to drift in the air without flapping wings

tendon: one of the parts of the body that join muscles to bones

For More Information

Books

Alderfer, Jonathan. *National Geographic Kids Bird Guide of North America*. Washington, DC: National Geographic, 2013.

Amstutz, Lisa J. *Rain Forest Animal Adaptations*. Mankato, MN: Capstone Press, 2012.

Danielson, Ethan. *Inside Bird Nests*. New York, NY: PowerKids Press, 2016.

Websites

Project Beak
projectbeak.org
Get an in-depth look at bird adaptations, including photos and fun facts.

San Diego Zoo Kids: Birds
kids.sandiegozoo.org/animals/birds
Cool pictures and information teach you all about birds.

Publisher's note to educators and parents: Our editors have carefully reviewed these websites to ensure that they are suitable for students. Many websites change frequently, however, and we cannot guarantee that a site's future contents will continue to meet our high standards of quality and educational value. Be advised that students should be closely supervised whenever they access the Internet.

Index

Arctic tern 26
beak/bill 12, 18, 19, 28
bee hummingbird 6
birds of paradise 23
bones 16
calls 25
camouflage 9
display 23, 28
eastern screech owl 9
Emperor penguins 29
feathers 8, 9, 10, 11, 12, 13, 15, 16, 23, 28
feet 20, 21
gizzard 17
habitat 4, 8
herons 20
largest bird 7

migrate 27
mockingbirds 24
ostrich 7
peacocks 22
predators 7, 9, 24, 25
preening 12
prey 8, 18
raptors 18
robins 15, 21
smallest bird 6
snowy owls 8
songs 24
species 4, 25, 28
toes 20, 21, 28
toucans 19
turkeys 14
wings 10, 11, 14, 15